Falling in Soul-Full Love Tips
Book 1 - Beginnings

Two Hearts...Into One!

The Soul-Full Love School™
www.Soul-FullLove.School

By
Christina Balingbing
and
Cary Grant Anderson

Falling in Soul-Full Love Tips – Book 1

Copyrights Page

This book and its Tips contents are copyright 2017 by Cary Grant Anderson and the Soul-Full Love School™, www.Soul-FullLove.School, a school of Leonardo da Vinci Minds University run by The DaVinci Minds, Inc. a non-profit educational and research organization.

Please share these Tips and their posters and memes freely with everyone on your website, emails, Facebook page, printed page, etc.

Just make sure that the following copyright statement and attribution is included on all Tips, posters, memes, and other materials produced by our school:

**Copyright 2017 Cary Grant Anderson and
The Soul-Full Love School™**
www.Soul-FullLove.School
a School of Leonardo da Vinci Minds University™
www.LeonardoDaVinciMinds.University

Happy Sharing and Loving!

- Christina Balingbing and
- Cary Grant Anderson

Falling in Soul-Full Love Tips – Book 1

Contents

Copyrights Page 2

Fore Words... 6

Chapter 1 – Introduction 9

Chapter 2 – Daily Love Duties 14

   Tip #1: Have Daily Love Duties....................................... 15

   Tip #2: Be a Goddess Worshipper! 17

   Tip #3: Do Your Daily Love Duties 20

   Tip #4: Always Hold Hands... 21

   Tip #5: Always Touch 23

   Tip #6: Make Your Touch…Gentle, Random, and Seductive 25

   Tip #7: The One-Minute Surprise Hug and Hold.......... 27

   Tip #8: Standing and Sitting Touching.......................... 29

   Tip #9: Sensual Touching in Passing............................. 30

   Tip #10: Always Being a Real Man 32

   Tip #11: Always Being a Real Woman.......................... 34

   Tip #12: Always Sensually Touch and Snuggle............. 35

   Tip #13: Snuggle in the Morning after Waking 37

   Tip #14: Snuggle in the Evening before Sleeping......... 39

   Tip #15: Talk About Each Day. Open Communication is a Must 42

   Tip #16: Trust Your Partner at all Times, Ask When in Doubt 45

Falling in Soul-Full Love Tips – Book 1

Tip #17: Constantly Admire & Inspire Each Other 47

Tip #18: Cook His/Her Favorite Meal 50

Chapter 3 – Weekly Musts 53

Tip #19: Have Weekly Musts... 54

Tip #20: Thursday Night Date Night............................. 56

Tip #21: Getaway Weekends 58

Tip #22: Build a Hobby Together.................................. 59

Chapter 4 – True Romance 62

Tip #23: Work to Have…And to Keep… True Romance 63

Tip #24: Write a Poem Regularly on a Card 65

Tip #25: Flowers and a Short Poem on a Random Basis 67

Tip #26: Dancing Whenever and Wherever "Our Song" is Heard 69

Tip #27: Do Something Together Night (No Phone, TV, or Internet).. 70

Tip #28: Rainy Day Scenarios 72

Tip #29: Public and Private Displays of Affection 74

Tip #30: Random Kisses - Different Times and Parts of the Body 76

Tip #31: Secret Elevator Kisses..................................... 78

Chapter 5 – Honoring the Goddess (Woman) 80

Tip #32: Acknowledge the Goddess in Your Woman... 85

Tip #33: Look Your Woman in Her Eyes....................... 88

Tip #34: Eye Gazing…And Finding Her Soul in Her Eyes 90

Tip #35: Do Every Day Goddess Honoring 93

Falling in Soul-Full Love Tips – Book 1

    Tip #36: Make her a Central Part of your Life 94

Chapter 6 – Honoring the Godden (Man) 96

    Tip #37: Acknowledge the Godden in Your Man 98

    Tip #38: Look Your Man in His Eyes 99

    Tip #39: Eye Gazing…Finding His Soul in His Eyes 100

    Tip #40: Every Day Godden Honoring 102

    Tip #41: Make him a Central Part of your Life 104

    Tip #42: Be Attentive to his Needs 106

    Tip #43: Become his Best Friend and Lover 108

    Tip #44: Trust his Capability to Provide 110

    Tip #45: Be Loyal to him 112

Chapter 7 – Putting It All Together 115

    Tip #46: Slow and Steady 117

    Tip #47: Only One (or Two) Tips a Week! 119

    Tip #48: Make Each Tip a Habit 120

    Tip #49: Restart Forgotten Tips Occasionally 121

    Tip #50: Ride Through the Bumps in the Road 122

    Tip #51: Forever is Long Time…There is No Hurry 123

    Tip #52: Enjoy the Journey! 124

After Words 125

About the Soul-Full Love School™ 126

About the Triple Heart Logo 127

About the Authors 128

The Tips Book and Course Series 130

Fore Words

This is a simple book of simple tips to bring Soul-Full Love into your life.

What is Soul-Full Love?

Soul-Full Love is love that is so deep, pure, and strong that it comes from and touches and binds the Souls of two people together. It is the best type of Love and the highest level of Love.

And it's actually quite easy to achieve. But what's happening in our world nowadays is movement away from the basic thinking and behavior that leads away from Soul-Full Love to...Disastrous love.

We could write many, many books on Disastrous love...

But a better use of our time and your time is to write about the path to rich, deep, and rewarding Love – Soul-Full Love.

Falling in Soul-Full Love Tips – Book 1

Because that's what The Soul-Full Love Arts is all about: Finding your way to Soul-Full Love.

So here, in this simple and to the point book, we're going to list and discuss some very simple things that you and yours can do to nurture love that it may grow and one day turn into Soul-Full Love.

All of these tips in this book we have all done in our own lives. And we'll tell you the stories about how and when we did them. These tips are very simple, and sometimes unconventional, and sometimes potentially embarrassing (dancing in public!) but each and every one can be easily and simply done by you and yours. We did them…And so can you!

These tips are simple…And powerful…And will set you and your loved one on the path to wonderful physical love, then Spirit-Full Love, and then on to Soul-Full Love.

All you have to do is to try a tip a day and just work your way through all the tips in this book.

It's simple…And it's Fun!!!

What is NOT in this Book

The Tips in this book are based upon Grant's and Tina's own personal practices and experiences. We just didn't "borrow" them from other books. We live and have lived this Tips and we know that they work and are very powerful for Soul-Full Love. The Tips in this book are meant to help you and your progress towards and to Soul-Full Love. So, you will NOT see old, time worn, non-Soul-Full tips like "Buy her two dozen roses", "Buy her expensive jewelry", "Take her to an expensive restaurant", "Make yourself a slave to your man", and so forth.

Falling in Soul-Full Love Tips – Book 1

Tip #0 – There is an inverse (opposite) relationship between the Soul-Full-Ness of your relationship and the amount of money you have to spend or receive. The Soul cannot be bought.

Money + Expensive Gifts ≠ Soul-Full Love

So, in this book we skip all that bull crap. Money isn't Soul-Full. In fact, it often becomes the sole focus and center of a person's life…And then it becomes Soul Destroying. Just check out the lives and relationships of people who win the lottery or suddenly acquire a large amount of money. Having money and having Soul-Full Love is a very great Challenge. Expensive gifts are not Soul-Full. Spending time together and small inexpensive and meaningful personal gifts are.

We don't focus on gifts here in this first book of Tips. There are a few gifts of the Heart and Soul mentioned such as writing a poem or sending a card to your Love. It's the contents and the Soul-Full Expression that counts.

Practice being Soul-Full in your Love, and in your Life, and you will achieve Soul-Full Love.

- Cary Grant Anderson and Christina Balingbing

Chapter 1 – Introduction

So why another book of Love (and romance) tips?

Because all the books you've read so far have had little useful pieces here and there but really lack the "big picture" of what Love is all about and how to keep it and grow it.

Notice that we spell "Love" with a capital "L". That's because there's 2 types of love: love with a lower case "l" and Love with a capital "L".

How are they different? Imagine being deep in the desert and sitting on a rock and eating a dinner of an old K ration bar from World War II. It tastes really poorly but it does have essential nutrients for your body. It doesn't fill you up. It doesn't satisfy you. It's not what you want to keep eating...

Now imagine the opposite: You're ushered into a wonderful dining hall with windows overlooking a fountain gushing water high into the air and overlooking a beautiful green vista of rolling hills and mountains. You're escorted to a linen covered table with esquire china and real silver silverware where you're pleasantly surprised to find a very attractive dinner companion waiting for you. You find a sumptuous buffet of incredible foods and dishes are yours for dining and you also find your companion very, very interested in you and you have a wonderful conversation and a wonderful dinner...

Sitting on a rock in the desert with a K ration bar and dining with the lizards and cactuses is love with a lower case "l".

Dining with a wonderful companion in the dining hall of limitless dishes is Love with a capital "L".

So how do you get to that wonderful dining hall and to Love with a capital "L"?

To get to Love you have to walk the Path of Love.

These tips will help you get there.

Simply try these tips one at a time one a day or one a week and work at mastering them.

They don't always come naturally because of the ways which we've been brought up but keep at them.

Try one. Then another.

And you know what?

You're going to find that they are really fun!

And that Love with a capital "L" doesn't really take working at this or that.

It takes finding the fun, the happiness, and the joy in doing these simple little things that will put you on the Path to Soul-Full Love.

So, the first thing you have to do is to have an open mind.

Many people who think that they have an open mind actually do not. This is due to many reasons but mostly what happens in our life molds us in ways that often do not help us in life. If you grew up with a mother and father that loved, you and loved each other and showed that each and every day then you're in great shape for this book! If, however, you're like me (Grant) and grew up in a household without love then this book can be quite a challenge for you.

And, if you've been hurt in Love once or twice, then overcoming the Fear and Trust issues is going to take some effort and time too.

But...The Journey is worth it!

Falling in Soul-Full Love Tips – Book 1

And to Journey…And to get to your Destination…You have to put forth effort and take risks.

And the second thing you have to do in preparing to use these tips effectively is to "loosen up"!

This can be a challenge. It took me (Grant) a couple of decades to loosen up…But then all the techniques and practices in this book came quite naturally to me.

So…Relax and Try!!!

And the third thing you have to then do is to read through the tips and pick one to try today.

And I mean today!!!

This is not a book to put on your shelf!

This is a book to carry with you every day in your briefcase, your backpack, or your purse trying and re-trying first one tip and then another and then another until you've tried them all and mastered them all.

Then and only then you put the book on your shelf…With a big smile!

For once you've mastered each of these tips then you will be one happy and satisfied person!

So…Let's get started!!!

"Love is such a beautiful gift

That must be freely given.

For without Love,

Life is not worth living."

-Unknown

Chapter 2 – Daily Love Duties

Grant Quote:

> *"The best things in life are nearest: Breath in your nostrils, light in your eyes, flowers at your feet, duties at your hand, the path of right just before you. Then do not grasp at the stars, but do life's plain, common work as it comes, certain that Daily Love Duties and daily bread are the sweetest things in life."*
>
> - *Robert Louis Stevenson*

Tip #1: Have Daily Love Duties

Grant:

I call them "My Daily Love Duties". Things that I endeavor to do each and every day.

Now...You might think that My Daily Love Duties are simple things like always flossing after meals or taking time to say a prayer or even keeping an up to date things to do list...But those are not the "Daily Love Duties" that I'm talking about.

The Daily Love Duties that I'm talking about are very important. And very fulfilling. And very fun. I think that it's very, very important for me to do each and every day. Why? Well, er, ah, I have a special secret...

I don't like telling people about it because they think I'm weird. Or crazy. Or some weird and crazy Pagan non-Christian person. Well, I'm not a Pagan. But I'm not a Christian either. I certainly don't consider myself crazy. (Actually, I had myself checked a few years back and, yep, I'm definitely not crazy. Yea!) As for weird, I think that's relative. People who do not acknowledge and respect femininity and women I think are weird. Actually, I think that there is something wrong with them. That most men don't respect women is rather obvious. Most men think women are less than men, inferior, although most don't come right out and say it.

I'm different. I think that women are actually superior to men in many ways. Women have a depth and a presence of Soul that I find very lacking in men. I think that women are developing faster than men and will in a few decades overtake them in many ways. This is already happening in American schools where female students are scoring higher and higher over the male students.

Now, don't get me wrong. I'm not a feminist. Nor am I very supportive of much of the Feminist agenda because I don't believe that it honors women but instead tries to make them behave as men. Which I think is a great step backwards. I also think that Femininity is disappearing in America and Western Civilization in favorite of "plastic-ness" where woman is defined by how much make up she wears, the ridiculously uncomfortable clothes she also wears, and how she acts more like a guy than a gal.

Ok, so you see a little bit about where I'm coming from.

I'm not here to debate things. I'm just telling you where I'm coming from.

Tip #2: Be a Goddess Worshipper!

And now it's time for me to come out of the root cellar and tell you my little big secret:

"I'm a Goddess Worshipper!"

Huh? You mean Grant that you're a Pagan or something?

No, I'm not a Pagan. Or a member of any religion old or new.

I'm just a guy that sees the Goddess in every woman. Most especially in my Woman. The woman who is at my side being my companion and my partner in life.

For I believe that what's inside a woman is much more valuable than her external wrappings.

A woman's Soul, a good woman's Soul, is what's important to me. And I only want to be with a woman with a good Soul.

And then I want to acknowledge and honor it whenever I'm around her.

I call this "Worshipping" because to me it's kind of like worshipping a Goddess.

While this may upset some overly religious folk it's actually what I think of as "Honoring" but people in America and elsewhere don't really understand what Honoring is all about. I'll talk more about this in an upcoming chapter about Honoring the Goddess and the Godden in a relationship and each other.

But for now, you can just think of my Goddess Worshipping as Honoring the Goddess Essence in the Woman who is at my side sharing my life.

And that's where my Daily Love Duties come in.

I guess that someone might call it "Daily Devotional Duties" and that's perhaps a good name too but I call it my Daily Love Duties because I feel and believe that it is my responsibility to show, demonstrate, and act out my Love for my Woman each and every day.

Thus...My Daily Love Duties to show my love.

And that's what we have here now: I'm going to tell you my Tips about how I show my Love to my Woman each and every day.

And then Tina is going to tell you about her Tips for the same. These things come naturally to a woman, so she doesn't have a name for them. Because it's just second nature for a feminine woman in touch with her Soul.

Us guys have to learn these things and practice them a lot in order to get them right.

And the most important thing to realize is: I ENJOY doing these things! And you can too!

Falling in Soul-Full Love Tips – Book 1

When you see the smile on her face and the Love in her eyes and you feel her heart touch yours...Then you'll Know!

So...Let's get started with Grant's Daily Love Duties!!!

Tip #3: Do Your Daily Love Duties

Grant has 3 simple Daily Love Duties that he endeavors to do each and every day with his Love.

They are Whenever Possible:

1. Always Hold Hands.
2. Always Touch.
    a. When passing each other.
    b. When standing or sitting next to each other.
3. Always Sensually Touch and Snuggle.
    a. Snuggle in the Morning after waking.
    b. Snuggle in the Evening before sleeping.

These are things which are quite easy to do. You don't have to buy anything. You don't have to set up a reminder in your calendar to do these. You don't have to have the discipline to get up at dawn and jog 20 miles in the dark....

All you have to do is...Just do them!!!

Let's walk you through them!

Tip #4: Always Hold Hands

Are you standing beside your Love?

Ok, take her hand and hold it. It will soon become automatic.

Are you standing close to your Love?

Ok, move closer and take her hand unless she needs it for driving or something.

If you can't take her hand, then rest your hand on her arm or leg or side or wherever whenever possible.

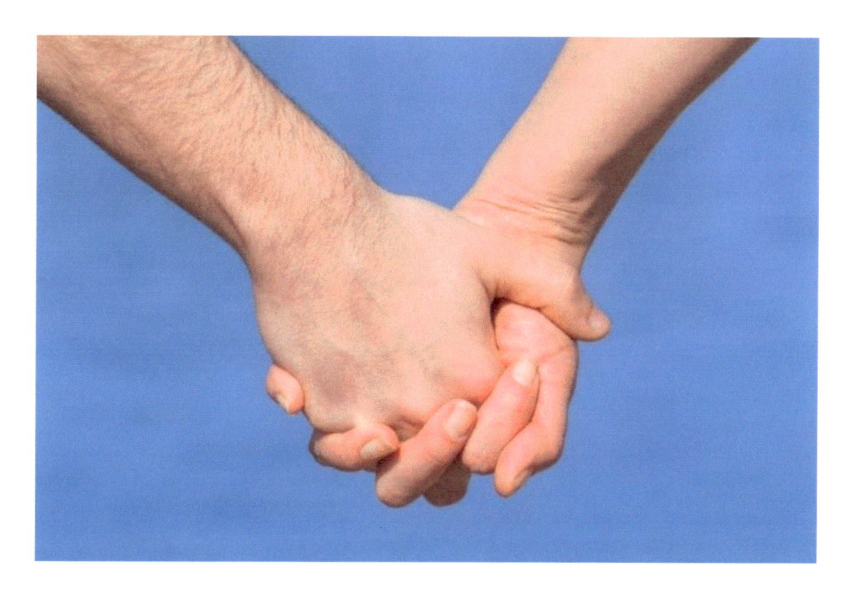

It's this simple!

Heck, even I eventually figured it out!

Falling in Soul-Full Love Tips – Book 1

And…There's no excuse for not doing this!

I used to walk around in public with a wife that was some years younger than me. I always held her hand. I got dumped by a wonderful woman who was 10 or more years older than me. If she'd of had me as her man I'd have been walking around holding her hand in public.

So…Get over it! There's no real excuse! Just do it with Love and nothing else matters!!!

Falling in Soul-Full Love Tips – Book 1

Tip #5: Always Touch

Did you just walk past your Love?

Did you touch Her? No? Why NOT?

You just missed an excellent Touch Opportunity!!!

Now, it's very, very simple. You walk past your Love and you touch her in passing.

Lightly. Affectionately. Simply.

Each time you Touch her you are telling her that you Love, Honor, and Respect Her.

So, do it EACH TIME you walk past Her!

Try it! DO IT!!! It's such a simple thing! And to a Good Woman it says much, much more than a dozen roses or a shopping spree.

(Tina: So true! A Good Woman's happiness doesn't really depend on material things. A dozen roses and a shopping spree are great! But when she becomes used to it, she will soon realize she is empty inside. Material

happiness doesn't last long. But when a man provides her with lots of Love and Care and Intimacy, she is filled inside with a Love so True and she becomes more Loving and Loyal to her man.)

Now...Let's go on to the 2nd more advanced part of this:

Tip #6: Make Your Touch...Gentle, Random, and Seductive

This means that when you walk past her, you touch her Gently but also firstly Randomly. You vary where and how you touch her. On your first pass during the day, touch her on her upper behind just below the waist. Use one finger, two fingers, three fingers, or all of your fingertips. The most important thing here is that it is Gentle and Random. You vary where and how you touch her.

You do something like this:

1. <u>First Pass:</u> Brush your fingertips along the backside of her behind just below her waist. Note: This is assuming that you pass in back of her. If needed, vary how you pass her, in front, behind, to the side, going across the room just so that you can pass her and touch

her. Each time you do this you Honor Her and she'll smile.
2. Second Pass: Using one finger, trace a gentle line down her upper arm from her shoulder to by her elbow.
3. Third Pass: Brush three fingers up her side of her torso upwards and arching across her back a bit (assuming you're in back of her).
4. Fourth Pass: Reach up and Gently touch her cheek. Or her ear. Or the hollow under her jaw.
5. Fifth Pass: Place your hand on her shoulder and give a little Gentle squeeze in passing.
6. Sixth Pass: Brush the back of your hand against her back.
7. Seventh Pass: Briefly and Gently touch her upper thigh.
8. Eighth Pass: Briefly and Gently touch her side as you pass.
9. Ninth Pass: Now you surprise her and stop as you are about to pass her. Touch her gently on her shoulders and kiss her gently on her cheek...Or neck...Or forehead...Or elsewhere. Vary it! Randomize it!
10. Tenth Pass: Walk PAST her slightly, stop, and reach back and Gently touch her somewhere then continue your walking.

ALWAYS RANDOMIZE THE TIMING, THE PLACEMENT, AND THE TYPE OF TOUCH!

ALWAYS KEEP HER GUESSING!!!

This makes it a personal challenge. And a very pleasant game to play!!!

Tip #7: The One-Minute Surprise Hug and Hold

And don't forget to throw in the One Minute Surprise Hug and Hold too!

Walk up to her and put your arms around her and don't say anything. Just close your eyes and hug her then hold her close for a minute. Or longer. If she asks you why at first just tell her that you wanted to. Then hug and hold her some more.

(Tina: I love this part. It feels so romantic! Ladies, when your Man does this to you, two things you could do. First, when he is behind you wrapping his arms around you, touch his arms wrapped around you with your left hand and with your right hand touch his face on the cheek or his neck and move his face closer to your face, and with your

eyes closed, feel his embrace. Second, whether he holds you from behind or front, hug him back by embracing and wrapping your arms around him. Rest your head on his chest and with eyes closed, feel his heart beat. Then, you could surprise him too by giving him a kiss!)

Soon she'll be looking forward to the Hug and Holds.

And you will be too!

Tip #8: Standing and Sitting Touching

When you are standing or sitting next to your Love...ALWAYS touch her. Always connect physically with her. Hold her hand. Rest your hand on her arm or leg. ALWAYS physically connect.

Falling in Soul-Full Love Tips – Book 1

Tip #9: Sensual Touching in Passing

Remember I said to randomize how you touch your Love when you walk past her?

And did you notice that I didn't include any, uh, "naughty" areas in my descriptions and instructions?

There's a reason for that.

First you must master the Gentle Passing Touch.

And it must be non-sexual.

That's so that she knows that you're honoring Her as a woman and not just signaling for sex.

Falling in Soul-Full Love Tips – Book 1

But when you're in private...And you wouldn't mind having sex...Then Gently Touch in Passing her special parts:

- A. Run your fingers along her behind.
- B. Touch her upper inner thigh below her behind.
- C. Touch the side of her breast.
- D. Touch the underneath area of her breast.

Notice that this gets more challenging!

You're going have to practice at this and be fast and quick at it.

While I don't recommend doing this in public or when there are others about...I've been known to glance around quickly then steal a Touch along her behind when no one else is looking.

This is "risqué" and playful and extends the game of Touching into a more challenging level.

Tip #10: Always Being a Real Man

But use this sparingly and randomly because it's only in the bedroom that you're really going to be worshipping and Honoring on a very intimate level.

But controlling your manly lustful urges and desires is mandatory. For if you cannot then you aren't really a man. You're just a weakling.

To be a Real Man you have to be able to control yourself and be strong enough to be sensual not sexual. And intimate not bestial. And caring rather than being a jerk or jackass or an unfeeling idiot.

Because if you have any brains at all it should be dawning on you now that all this touching stuff is going to take you and her to a much more physical and touching level.

And what you really, really want but can't put into words is that that is exactly what you really want: To be Touched, to be Held, and to be Loved.

(Tina: I agree. I believe each and every one has this goal in life. However only a few has yet attained and knows how to truly Love. But it's never too late to learn! And that's what this Tips book is teaching about.)

So be strong and be courageous.

And be a Real Man and be Really Loved.

Tip #11: Always Being a Real Woman

When you are truly In Love, sometimes the feeling is overwhelming and controlling. It seems you are on "cloud 9" as they call it, and you just want to go with the flow of an overwhelming emotion. This is good but dangerous to some extent.

You should enjoy the feeling but be on guard, take extra precautions, especially if it's on the early stages of your relationship. You need to get to know your man fully, so you should be cautious.

Touching and cuddling is good, but it usually leads to a more romantic sex. Be sure with yourself that you truly want this man before diving into a sexual intimacy. Make sure your man knows the boundaries of your relationship. Be open with him. Make him realize (by telling him frankly) that you're not into a one-night stand with him but you wanted a long-term relationship with commitment.

It takes a lot of self-control and courage to be in control of yourself. But once you have the assurance that you can fully trust him, then there's nothing to be afraid of. Just enjoy being you and being with him. Be true to yourself, be cautious but do not deny your man with the intimacy he needs. Every human being needs a human touch and intimacy at some level. Only when you truly Love him that you can easily provide that need.

Tip #12: Always Sensually Touch and Snuggle

When I talk about "sensually" I mean to touch and snuggle more intimately whenever and wherever possible.

And that really means in private of course.

So...When you're in privacy with your Love then sensually touch and snuggle.

This means that this does not lead to sex...At least most times...But is just a nice way to connect physically and intimately.

Hmmmm....Okay, guys! Some of you have no idea what I'm talking about and think that touching is just a prelude to sex. Well it's not. Sure, sex starts with touching. But

Falling in Soul-Full Love Tips – Book 1

there's an entire level of intimacy that goes beyond sex. I know that it's very hard for some of you to understand but please keep working on it. And women...Please help your men understand by showing them and being patient with them. Men can be such Neanderthals and it can take them some time to learn these important things!

Ok, now let's get back to talking about Sensual Touch and Snuggle.

Sensual means physical and intimate but doesn't really mean sex.

So...Being sensual means that I can touch a woman anywhere on Her body with Love and Affection and Gentleness but without a demand for sex.

If you need to, go slow and practice this bit by bit snuggling on the couch watching a movie or better yet in bed...

Tip #13: Snuggle in the Morning after Waking

I used to do this every morning with my ex-Filipina wife. She wasn't a natural cuddler, so she couldn't/wouldn't snuggle up to me and sleep while touching in a snuggling/cuddling position. So...The alarm would go off and I'd reach out an arm and slap the snooze button. Then I'd turn over and work my way over to her side of the bed and take her in my arms and hold her and nuzzle her head and neck...

Nine minutes later the alarm goes off again!

I move over and reach out and slam the snooze button again.

Back to snuggling!

Falling in Soul-Full Love Tips – Book 1

Nine minutes later the alarm goes off again!

Some days this goes on one or two more times.

Other days I kiss her head and turn the alarm off and get ready for work.

But what I've done is just told her in my actions how much I Love her and value her. And I've grabbed 20 minutes (ok, actually 18 minutes) of wonderful snuggling cuddling time with a beautiful sensual woman in bed!

Wow!!! What a way to start the morning!!!

(Tina: Indeed, a good way to start the morning! Ladies, coming from a man (Grant) - Take Note!! And make sure to inspire your man each and every day. We fuel their energy and daily moods by our actions too. When they are happy in the morning, I'm sure they will be eager and can't wait to get home to you in the evening!

It's also a great time to have a pillow talk while cuddled together. But make sure you talk only about good things that happened during the day. Better yet, this is the best time to flirt with your Love. Be playful and fun especially in the morning to boost you and your-Man's energy level!)

Tip #14: Snuggle in the Evening before Sleeping

And I used to do this too every night.

Before sleeping, whether or not we had sex (most nights it was after evening sex!), I would wrap her in my arms and hold her and snuggle/cuddle up to her for 20 minutes or a bit longer. Then I'd turn over and go to sleep.

I'd really prefer to hold her while I slept but she wasn't a sleeping cuddler/snuggler. And I have had to use a VPAP machine to keep me breathing during the night since I have CSA (Central Sleep Apnea) where my body forgets to breathe when I sleep. So, the machine keeps me alive at night and I have to wear a breathing mask connected to it. I call it my Darth Vader Breath Mask for fun and it's a pain but it's much better than the alternative of never being able to sleep or dying in my sleep. This interferes with snuggling and cuddling while sleeping but I work around this limitation with my 20 Minute Morning and Evening Snuggles.

That's just what you have to do: Work around any obstacles or problems. Love will find a way.

True Love always finds a way…

And Tina always covers the things that I miss…

Tina Quote:

> "Love is not a Destiny, but a Journey of a Lifetime. It's not how much Love we have in the beginning, but how much Love we build until the end."
> - Author Unknown

Tina:

Grant has uncovered the very touching and endearing ways of Loving your partner. I actually loved them all, especially the cuddling/snuggling just for the purpose of doing it. It would be more fun doing it especially on rainy/cold days! (I just love cuddles! ☺)

And Thanks Grant, for saying that men are honoring their women by doing so. Not all men may still be doing them, but aside from honoring their women, it's really a good way to connect to your Loved One. So, it's great to start doing them now! The fun thing is, not only men but women also could initiate doing them!

Now, I am here to uncover more and other 'Daily Love Duties' that we, women, are already doing them unconsciously since they are natural to us, but sometimes we tend to let go when we become focused on other things. This is just more of a reminder, in case we now forget. And to some men, who sometimes find it difficult to understand their women, I am uncovering the reasons for you. So, this is also for you... something good to know and worth doing.

Tip #15: Talk About Each Day. Open Communication is a Must

Ever been with someone who doesn't talk much?

Isn't it annoying when sometimes you don't know what's on his mind?

You sometimes feel he is hiding something and doesn't really want you to know. And when you ask, he would respond quite a bit or none at all! For us women, this is so frustrating and annoying!

For the relationship to grow, good communication is a must. At best, daily.

Be open to your partner. S/He has all the right to know whatever is on your mind.

Falling in Soul-Full Love Tips – Book 1

Don't hide secrets from your other half. When you try to be un-communicative, it will lead to doubt and mistrust. But when you open up everything to each other, you become more trusting to one another.

Remember the days you started dating, you always wanted to talk to each other. You always wanted to know what's going on with him/her.

It feels like everyday information you know about each other, even the little ones, are significant! And you also feel, you wanted to tell him/her everything about you.

Every day is an opportunity for a good communication. (Grant: Great Point!) *Don't let each day pass without talking to your partner.*

It's one way of showing you care about each other. And it's a wonderful feeling when someone cares to know what's going on with you!

With constant communication, you are building the trust, getting to know each other deeper and becoming more connected to one another.

As a final note, always be honest and keep communication lines open. Always let your partner know what's on your mind. There is nothing to hide. (Grant: And everything to gain!)

(Grant: Guys...I know that it can be a challenge to talk...But remember as Tina says about talking a lot when dating...And work on listening without fixing. Women want to talk to "let off steam" and "to connect". You will tend to try to fix things that are talked about. Women don't want this...They just want someone to listen to them. I know it's not natural for you. But try listening and not fixing!)

Tip #16: Trust Your Partner at all Times, Ask When in Doubt

I could say, "Trust is the foundation of True Love". When you Love someone, you are entrusting your whole self and heart to him/her. You are confident that s/he will take care of it.

It's not easy to completely trust someone who was once a stranger. Especially in the early stages of relationships, it's always necessary to communicate. Don't hide your feelings, always ask when in doubt.

Women have this thing called "basic instinct". It's a feeling that you instantly feel when your partner is doing something behind your back. It's like you know something's wrong but you can't exactly pinpoint what it is.

So you become uneasy and suspicious. Sometimes the feeling of doubt may be true to what is happening but there are times it could just be born out of jealousy. In such instances, women are most often conclusive and judgmental.

(Grant: Guys this is where women are definitely superior! They have this natural sensing ability...It comes from their Heart and Soul...So get used to it. And open up! It's perfectly ok to talk about your feelings and fears. It takes a courageous man, a Real Man, to do so!)

There is no better way than to directly ask your partner. But make sure that both of you are in a pleasant mood.

The best time to talk about sensitive matters is while you are doing some low energy activities (like siesta) and both are calm.

If possible, hold your partner's hand and talk in a low voice. When things get rough, STOP and let things cool down a bit then deal with the issue again when you are both calm and ready to talk.

Tip #17: Constantly Admire & Inspire Each Other

When you admire your partner's special qualities and abilities, it touches both your hearts.

In one way or another, it connects you more in a special way. The husband that is admired by his wife grows more confident and inspired to do his task. The wife that is admired by her husband becomes a more loving and loyal wife.

For the husband:

1. Admire your wife for taking care of your children.

2. Admire her for maintaining a clean home.
3. Admire her for keeping your things tidy and organized.
4. Admire her for keeping the budget and being a wise spender.
5. Admire her ability to cook.
6. Admire her for helping you anytime you need her.
7. Admire her in every simple way.
8. (Grant: Admire and Honor her femininity.)

For the wife:

1. Admire your husband's accomplishments.
2. Admire his capability to do his job well.
3. Admire his strength and masculinity.
4. Admire his ability to cook.
5. Admire his willingness to help in the household chores.
6. Admire his ability to do carpentry and other manly works.
7. Admire him in every simple way.

When you are admired, you become more inspired to do more and become better in what you do. Make your relationship grow with the constant admiration of each other.

Sometimes you may never know what's going on in the minds and hearts of each other. Sometimes your man's ego may have been hurt by his boss or someone at work. When *you praise him, it will boost his ego and he will be inspired to achieve and do more.*

On the other hand, the wife may have been too tired from all the household works. When the husband comes home and admires even the simplest meal from his wife, her tiredness is lifted up and there is a glow from within.

(Grant: Wow! This is very well said! And very important!)

(Grant: Guys, when a woman makes a meal for me or does some little thing for me like gets me a glass of water, I always tell her "Thank You!" Try this! It tells Her that you appreciate and admire Her!)

Tip #18: Cook His/Her Favorite Meal

There is a saying that "the way to a man's heart is through his stomach". That goes true with women also.

One way of pampering your other half is by doing something special for him/her. Cooking his/her favorite meal is one way to show your Love.

You could alternately do this with each other. If both are working and busy on weekdays, this becomes a "must do" on weekends.

You don't have to wait for special occasions to cook something for him/her!

It becomes more surprising and romantic if you do this even on ordinary days. Also, it doesn't have to be always the favorite meal. You could also come up with something of your own dish.

While the other is busy cooking or has done the cooking, you could help in the cleanup or washing of the dishes. Even with household chores, it's still a partnership. ☺

(Grant: And guys…Cook for her sometimes too! And if she cooks…Do the dishes! Oh! And don't forget to sneak up on her in the kitchen and touch and nuzzle her whenever you can!)

Falling in Soul-Full Love Tips – Book 1

"We come to Love not by

finding a perfect person,

But by learning to see an

imperfect person perfectly."

-Unknown

Chapter 3 – Weekly Musts

"The mass of men lead lives of quiet desperation..."
  - Henry David Thoreau

"Nowadays we all seem to live lives where we just struggle for survival...And drift slowly apart. Why don't we live Life for Love instead? And drift nicely into Soul-Full Love?"
  - Cary Grant Anderson

Tip #19: Have Weekly Musts

If you are both working and busy at work on week days, ALWAYS make time for each other on weekends. Never neglect your partner's happiness or your own over work.

As couples, you need to do something together. Aside from having a hobby to enjoy together, DO something together. Do something you both enjoy that will rekindle the romance or make you feel more connected to your partner.

It could be simply something like a stroll in the park or going to some nice beaches. It could be going to your favorite local restaurant where you order your favorite food (like pizza) or having a nice dinner date with your partner. You could also do your hobbies or read books together.

It doesn't have to be extremely extravagant. Just spend time being with your Love. Surely, both of you will be grateful for the time you spend together. And it will be something you'd always look forward to during the week.

Falling in Soul-Full Love Tips – Book 1

Tip #20: Thursday Night Date Night

When you were still dating, you always set aside a time to see each other. It would be by having a lunch or dinner somewhere or watching movies together.

The man would usually want to impress his woman by treating her to some expensive restaurants. But a Good Woman doesn't really care about the place; it is being with her man that she feels more important.

This is a very good practice and must be continued.

So ALWAYS have a "couple time". Date at least once a week. It could be anytime or any day of the week, but it's more romantic at night time. Grant suggests a Thursday

Night Date Night where there are less people out and you could have more time alone together.

It doesn't have to be an expensive date, but always make it a quality time together.

Tip #21: Getaway Weekends

Weekend is the best time of the week to have fun together and to connect more. Understand that weekdays could be busy days at work and you see each other few hours before and after sleep, so make sure you set aside the weekend for family or couple time.

Go somewhere and have fun!

It could be at the beach or some places with tourist attractions. Rent a room or house and stay over for the weekend. This is also a good opportunity to practice your Daily Love Duties to your partner.

If you have kids, it would be good to bring them along. But also set a time alone together.

Tip #22: Build a Hobby Together

Do something together, do something you both love doing. The more you'll become connected as a couple if you do something together. It could be by sharing a similar hobby or you could simply do the household chores together.

A list of good hobbies to do together:
- *Gardening*
- *Cooking*
- *Biking*
- *Reading*
- *Writing*
- *Singing*
- *Dancing*
- *Playing instruments (i.e., flute, guitar, piano, violin, etc.)*
- *Workouts (i.e., Zumba, Yoga, etc.)*

- *And Many More!*

Do them on weekends since you have more time together. Try this and you'll always look forward to more weekends together!

"The best moments in my Life,

Are the moments spent with You."

-Author Unknown

Chapter 4 – True Romance

Have you ever been in love and felt like it's the most wonderful feeling ever? Feels like the world is such a beautiful paradise and it feels so magical that you want it to last forever.

Isn't it such a wonderful feeling? But how do you keep such wonderful excitement with your partner? How do you make it last?

Tip #23: Work to Have…And to Keep… True Romance

Being with someone you love is the most exciting and fulfilling feeling you'll ever have. Imagine being loved and pampered by your partner. Imagine being always excited seeing him/her. Imagine always being together and loving each other.

But all these take some efforts for both couples. Each one must work on making the relationship work. A romantic relationship is not a fairy tale. You don't just wait and let it happen. It's always a work in progress. It never stops. And don't let it stop. Keep the relationships going. Keep the romance alive.

Sometimes you may feel tired and may want to give up because your partner doesn't seem to cooperate or may seem distant at times. Sometimes also you or both of you might have "lost" the feeling. But don't panic. It's just temporary. We all feel that way. But we can always change all that. It just takes an extra little effort.

Us women always wants romance in a relationship. We are very touchy (most women) and can be easily pleased by some simple romantic gestures like holding hands, kissing, hugging and snuggling. For some men, it would already mean sex (as mentioned by Grant in previous tips), but some women just want to feel physically close to his man. And this is a very good way to bond and re-connect with your partner. It's as simple as that.

There are other simple ways you can do to keep a romantic relationship going. It will be revealed to you in the next tips…

Tip #24: Write a Poem Regularly on a Card

A Flower

A Flower
Is
A Moment in Time
Priceless
Endless...

A Flower
Is
To Behold
To Breathe
To Bespoke...

Sometimes what we feel is best expressed in poems or even songs.

The poem can be as short as 2 stanzas but the important thing is the message it conveys.

Falling in Soul-Full Love Tips – Book 1

If you cannot directly tell your partner what is in your heart, let your poems speak for you.

It is very endearing and romantic!

It will surely melt his/her heart and you'll soon get a positive response.

Aside from poems, it can also be song lyrics. Include a part of your favorite songs in a card to remind you and your partner. It could be in a card or an electronic card via email.

My boyfriend started doing this and I am touched. To me it feels like the lyrics are directly coming from his Heart and the song becomes more meaningful to me. The next time I heard the song, it reminds me of him. And I would stop and listen smiling.

Falling in Soul-Full Love Tips – Book 1

Tip #25: Flowers and a Short Poem on a Random Basis

Your Love

Your Love is not just what I wanted – it is what I needed
Your Love made me feel I am also important and wanted and needed
Your Love made me realize that Life would be much better with You
And now I couldn't live another day without ever thinking of You

Thank you for your Love, I will mostly cherish it
Thank you for your Time, I certainly appreciate it
Thank you for just being You, and always being there for me
I will always treasure your Love and keep it in my Heart, Forever
...

Falling in Soul-Full Love Tips – Book 1

A flower is a woman's weakness (it is for most women). She can't resist you if you bring her flowers.

Surprise her with her favorite flower/s and with a written note of endearment, which could be a few lines from a poem. Much better if you could make your own poem since it is most sincere coming from your heart.

They say that when you are truly in Love, you become inspired. Whatever comes from your heart is true.

It is easy to write a poem out of what you feel. The good thing is, you don't need to buy it. It's free! Both of you can make and share poems with each other. It's very endearing and romantic!

So, start making your own... it will surely inspire both you and your partner!

Tip #26: Dancing Whenever and Wherever "Our Song" is Heard

Lovers become more connected by a song that their hearts both recognize.

This is "Our Song" or others would call it a Love Song.

Whenever you hear it, it touches and connects you both in heart, mind and body. Dancing to the tune of it connects you both physically as your body touches.

Whenever the song is played, ask your partner for a dance and dance like nobody is watching.

(Grant: And, yes, I have done this many times in private and also in restaurants when we heard "Our Song". If it is truly "Our Song" then you just gotta do it!)

Tip #27: Do Something Together Night (No Phone, TV, or Internet)

Nowadays, the TV, internet or phone is becoming man's favorite toy or plaything. We sometimes give more time to it and neglect each other. I'm not saying you don't have to use these things but don't keep yourself glued or addicted to it. Instead of giving more time to it, just use it for its purpose.

I'm not a TV or internet-addict. I would watch TV for a couple of hours when everything has been taken care of, but usually I turn it on just to listen while I am doing other things and for the purpose of having someone talking at the background especially when I am alone at home. But oftentimes I would just turn on the music.

If you're a housewife and while your partner is away from work, you have all the time to yourself (a great time to improving oneself and the household). So that when he comes home, be sure to spend all your time and attention to him.

You could do something fun together every night. And I mean every night!

One Great Tip! You could give each other body massage. It's a great way to bond and connect to your partner, so simple yet enjoyable. You could do it in turns. Say, you give him the massage and he'll give you one after. If one is tired or not well, the other can give the massage and let him/her rest after. It's a very relaxing and enjoyable way of showing your Love and attention to your partner.

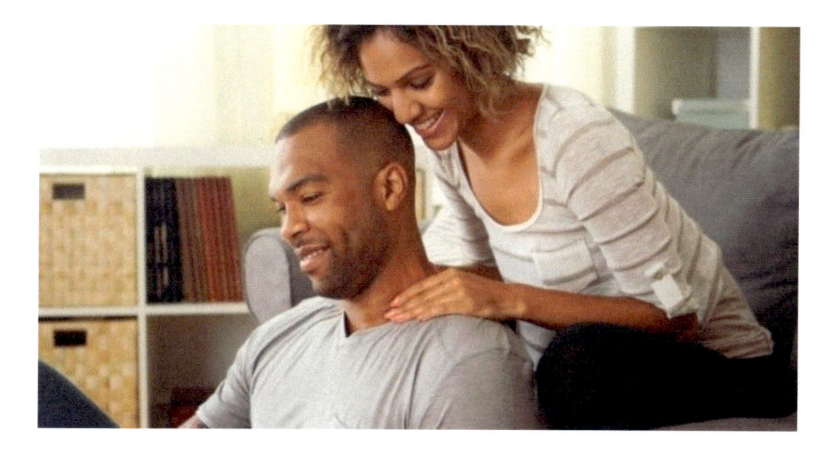

Tip #28: Rainy Day Scenarios

You can be romantic at any time of the day, but rainy day seems to bring a more romantic feeling.

While it's raining and cool outside, it's a good chance to snuggle next to your partner and cuddle. You could cuddle in the sofa but more fun in bed while you are both under the sheets.

While cuddled together, give each other some random kisses. You could also be playful and fun where you explore touching each other while your lips is locked in a kiss.

If you are both in the mood for more fun under the rain, go out and get wet. Feel like a child again and be playful with your partner. It all ends up in the shower together and a bedroom romance.

Tip #29: Public and Private Displays of Affection

Whether in public or private places, it's always good to show your Love for your partner. Being affectionate to your partner doesn't always have to be done in the privacy of your home.

When you are in public places, the more you need to show and display your affection to your partner because it's one way to announce your relationship and most important, is to make your partner feel that you are proud to be with him/her.

While in the privacy of your home, you can show affection in a lot different ways - from simple random touching to cuddling and kissing and ultimately to a sensually romantic love making.

However, it is more fun and challenging to do it in public. Just remember not to overdo your display of affection in public. Just do it in simple ways – like holding hands, touching, cuddling or kissing.

(Grant: Oh! And when your friends say something like, "Get a room!", meaning that you two should get a hotel room…Then you know that you're doing this good!)

Falling in Soul-Full Love Tips – Book 1

Tip #30: Random Kisses - Different Times and Parts of the Body

Kissing is one way to express Love and affection to your partner and can be considered the most important form of expression in a love relationship.

There are different types of kisses which you and your partner could experiment and explore – from traditional to passionate French kisses.

But the kiss doesn't only have to be on the lips or cheeks. Explore and try different ways.

Falling in Soul-Full Love Tips – Book 1

Vary and explore kissing on different parts of your partner's body. With kissing, you are also honoring your partner as your lips touches each part of the body. Be generous yet be gentle with your kisses.

Surprise each other with lots of kisses at different times.

Tip #31: Secret Elevator Kisses

Wouldn't it be thrilling and fun to be involved together in a short passionate kiss behind the elevator doors?

During those short moments of being alone together in the elevator gives the thrill to sneak a kiss with your partner.

A deep short passionate kiss can boost your man's libido and will make him want more. Be ready for longer intimate moments when you are both in the privacy of your home.

"For it was not into my ear you whispered,

but into my heart.

It was not my lips you kissed, but my Soul."

– Judy Garland

Chapter 5 – Honoring the Goddess (Woman)

Within every woman is a Goddess waiting to be discovered, nurtured and to bloom.

Knowing what a Goddess is…. And is not.

So, what is a Goddess?

The Goddess that I am referring to is the Goddess essence that is innately in every woman whether she realizes or honors it or not. The Goddess essence is automatically part of her Soul and defines who and what she truly is – A Goddess.

Most times she is a Goddess in Development having one or two or three or more of the Goddess traits (characteristics) as part of herself, and her characteristics and her life.

Too often a woman's Goddess essence and spirit is buried by bad social morals and customs. She is told as she grows up in a strict and man dominated world that she is inferior because she is a woman. That she has a "place" in the world and she must stay well within it. That she has a pre-ordained fixed role in life to play and that's it.

And all of these are wrong. Totally wrong.

Falling in Soul-Full Love Tips – Book 1

A woman is a proto-Goddess. She has all the inner foundations, the inner soul, to be a full and wonderful Goddess.

Yet, our societies do not see this at all. And work very hard to bury and hide such ideas and thoughts. And also to distract women into thoughts, ideas and paths that lead her away from her inner essence, her inner soul, and her ultimate destiny.

Consider what western culture now presents as a modern woman:

- Rich in money...
- Beautiful with cosmetics and plastic surgery...
- Narcissistic – lives only for herself...
- Expensive...
- Demand pampering money and gifts...
- Controlling to get what she wants...
- Materialistic-oriented...
- Shopping and gossip are most important things in her life...

Now consider what a normal and natural woman is like:

- Rich in Love and Life
- Beautiful within which shows in her eyes and smile.
- Full of empathy - lives for herself and her loved ones
- Not expensive – money is useful but not supremely important or required
- Demands integrity, honesty and Love.
- Cooperative to get what her kids, her spouse, then what she needs (although she often neglects this last part).
- Family and Love oriented.
- Family and Love and Happiness are the most important things in her life.

So which woman is a goddess?

The plastic, controlling, narcissistic bitch?

Or the loving, natural, family-oriented woman?

The goddess essence represents that natural femininity and female energy of the soul.

Including:
- Love
- Respect
- Honesty
- Integrity
- Small ego
- Self-sacrificing
- Empathy

The Goddess essence does **not** represent or include the opposite of these beautiful and wonderful traits. The cold-hearted narcissistic woman is neither beautiful nor admirable nor a goddess. Her so-called beauty is plastic and an illusion that never touches her eyes, her smile, her heart or her soul. She has no goddess traits. Just the opposite – she represents a desperate degeneration of the goddess essence and all she truly represents. You must look past the glitzy exterior. When you look inside, you'll find nothing but darkness, a cold and still heart, a soul that starved for love and light. And a great deep of unhappiness and despair desperately hidden by her ego and gaudy distractions of money.

Falling in Soul-Full Love Tips – Book 1

Contrast this with the natural woman of lesser money and means and lesser artificial beauty. When she loves, she loves with all her heart. Deep down to her soul. When she smiles, she lights up the darkness and dimness of our lives. She has her priorities straight in life. And these priorities of love, family and core values illuminate her soul in light and love. And feeds it the very things that all souls need and crave. She embraces her soul and feeds it with real love and real life each and every day in so many ways. And she and her soul both grow and develop.

Eventually into a goddess.

And while society and life often work to beat her down and bury her love and her budding Goddess-ness… it is always still there. Waiting to be touched. And nurtured.

And to blossom.

And that's your job as a man and her partner in life – to nurture and blossom her goddess essence.

Honoring the goddess in your woman is a 3-step process.

And here's some tips to help you with this:

1. Recognize the Goddess in her.
2. Acknowledge the Goddess in her.
3. Honor the Goddess in her.

Tip #32: Acknowledge the Goddess in Your Woman

Now that you've seen the Goddess essence in your woman, you must acknowledge it within your own mind and heart. Some people call this "believing" and that is a significant part of this process.

Sometimes you'll have to see it many times before you truly believe.

But first you must do something important.

- First, you must open your mind and heart to the possibility.
- Second, you must convince yourself by seeing it often enough to know that, Yes, you really did see it!
- And thirdly, you must admit it, at least to yourself.

Falling in Soul-Full Love Tips – Book 1

There's a recording that Grant recorded in the year 2001 that goes:

What Love is (simply):

Love is something completely different. Love is when her Soul touches your Soul. And your Soul touches hers. This is "Soul Touching". It is the start of and the basis of Real Love or Soul-full Love as we call it.

And eventually, continued, it will lead into real Soul-full Love with Soul Twynning. And the opening of many powers and abilities of Soul-full Love. And eventually transcendence. For when poets and people state that Love transcends all... They are right as it truly does.

So, that's the very quick overview of the Goddess essence and the Soul-full Love.

And you need it. And want it.

Why? Because your soul needs it. And wants it. As does hers.

But how to get started to get there?

Here's some more simple tips to get you started.

- Do every day Goddess honoring

- Keep looking every once in a while, to remind yourself

- Make her a central part of your life

If sports or beer is more important in your life than your woman, then you've missed the whole point here…

To Know
To Believe
To Do
Is
To Be!

So now that you know, and now that you believe, it is now time for you to "do".

In this context, the doing is … Honoring.

Tip #33: Look Your Woman in Her Eyes

You're a man.

You need to be able to look anyone straight and directly into their eyes.

And that includes your Woman, your Love.

Do it next time you see her.

It may seem a bit uncomfortable at first but after you see the Depth of her Love and a bit of her Soul in her eyes you will find that you enjoy it.

Falling in Soul-Full Love Tips – Book 1

You're a man.

Don't try to make excuses.

Don't be a wimp!

Be a Man and Look your Woman in her Eyes!

You will be glad you did!

(And weren't a wimp!)

> **Tip #34: Eye Gazing…And Finding Her Soul in Her Eyes**

Now that you can look your woman in her eyes we're going to go to the next step: Eye Gazing.

Eye Gazing, sometimes called "Soul Gazing" and other terms, is a very simple technique with big benefits. You can look deep, deep down into the "insides" of your woman…And see her Soul.

Many people are afraid of this – looking deep into another person's eyes. Why? Because of the deep closeness involved. What will I see in her? What will she see in me? If you are afraid of opening yourself up, then, well, you're going to have some reluctance to do this.

I can tell you, however, that you can make it through the initial uncomfortableness with just a little bravery. You're a man, right? So, you're supposed to have courage... and strength... and bravery. So, summon up a little bravery, be a man and do it. Don't be a wimp!

I've jumped out of aircraft at 14,000 feet (4,267 meters) and I can tell you that eye gazing doesn't need anywhere that level of courage or bravery. So, hold her hand and just do it!

What will you see?

You will at first see two eyes looking into yours...

Your eyes... her eyes... will tend to look away.

That's OK.

Just keep looking back into her eyes...

After a while you'll see some amazing things...

There will be a sudden depth in her eyes...

It's like looking into a deep well...

And you'll start seeing something else that it's hard to put words to...

That's her Spirit...

Meet her gaze with your gaze...

Falling in Soul-Full Love Tips – Book 1

And she will see into you also...

And see your Spirit...

To get to her Soul... And your Soul...

You must first meet her Spirit...

And her Yours as well...

Do eye gazing and you will deepen and strengthen your relationship and Love on your way to Soul-Full Love.

Try it!

And then you will know!

Tip #35: Do Every Day Goddess Honoring

If you've been trying and doing the Tips here in this book, then you are honoring the Goddess in your woman.

Doing one or more of these tips each and every day will "Do every day Goddess honoring".

This is very important so as to re-affirm and deepen your love each and every day. And avoid and combat the distractions, divergences and challenges that living in the everyday world presents us with daily.

Reconnect with your Lover, your mate each day. Pick one, two or three tips to do each and every day. My favorites are holding hands, the unexpected touches, and cuddling first thing and last thing each and every day.

Tip #36: Make her a Central Part of your Life

Your woman is your partner in life and in your trek to Soul-Full Love. So, treat her as a partner. Not as anything less.

You should know what is going on in her life. And her thoughts and feelings. You should be supportive and nurturing. But also brave enough to tell her when she needs to be corrected or when she is wrong.

The closer that you get towards a productive and supportive partnership, the closer and easier will be the path towards Soul-Full Love.

"Woman was taken out of man;

not out of his head to top him,

nor out of his feet to be trampled underfoot;

but out of his side to be equal to him,

under his arm to be protected,

and near his Heart to be Loved."

–inspired by Genesis 2:22-24.

Chapter 6 – Honoring the Godden (Man)

Remember Ladies, how we treat our men is very, very important...

If you treat him with respect, you will also earn respect.

But most importantly, you must admire him more than anyone else does. It doesn't only boost his ego, but gives him the confidence to become better and achieve more.

There is a saying that behind every success and failure of a man is a woman.

True! Unconsciously, we create their world... a woman can either make or break a man.

But the purpose of this book is to help us, women, make our men and build a better, stronger and more loving relationships.

So here goes my Tips on how you can build your man and Honor the Godden in him…

Tip #37: Acknowledge the Godden in Your Man

First and foremost, learn to acknowledge and find the Godden in your man. Within each man is a Godden hidden – ready and waiting to be discovered. It's deeply hidden within one's Soul. Most men are so good in hiding it probably because they've been hurt many times in the past. Only the right Soul can awaken it.

We all want to find our True Love but only a few finds them. It is because they never seek deeper. It is well hidden and is only found when you seek with your heart. With eyes closed to the physical flaws and well opened to what the heart holds.

For "it is only with the heart that one can see rightly; what is essential is invisible to the eye." – The Little Prince

Tip #38: Look Your Man in His Eyes

There's a saying that the eye is the window to one's soul. It's true. When you want to check a person's character, look straight into his/her eyes.

In similar manner, if you want to know whether your man is being honest with you, look into his eyes. If he can't look back straight into your eyes and feels a little discomfort, then something is wrong. He may tell you otherwise, but the eyes cannot lie, because the eye is the window to our soul. And the soul is basically honest in nature.

Falling in Soul-Full Love Tips – Book 1

Tip #39: Eye Gazing...Finding His Soul in His Eyes

Eye gazing is a powerful tool to connect. It is like looking at the very soul of your partner. It's a soul to soul connection.

Try doing this with your Love. It's the best technique to know how you feel for each other.

When you can't look into each other's eye, there's a big problem. Or when you feel emptiness when you look into his eyes, it's a big warning signal.

But when you look into his eyes and you can feel a wonderful feeling, that's when you've found him. It means both your souls acknowledge each other and recognizes the love within. The soul is trying to reach out and you'd feel your heart pumping fast and a surge of joy and excitement flows through your body.

And you felt like melting when he looks into your eyes. It's such a wonderful feeling.

Tip #40: Every Day Godden Honoring

"Wife you must submit to your husband..."

Aside from being a committed partner, keep your man happy by making him feel he is always the top priority. Although when kids come, he becomes next but make him feel you always have time for him.

Do not neglect your daily love duties. Always have a romantic time together. It will make him feel honored and it's one good way to boost his ego.

Aside from emotional connection, physical connection between couples is needed and necessary. Do not neglect your husband with this.

More than women, men need to feel physically connected and secured. It makes them happy when the physical need is met and it's a good way to bond with your partner.

Even when conflicts arise, do not neglect your man. Do not deprive him of this physical need. It's a good way to reconcile with your partner and to deeply connect.

From where I came, couples are usually reconciled when they make love.

As a woman, make the first move sometimes and this is just the perfect time to do it. Lower your pride. He is just waiting.

Men may have pride, but women have emotions. We can be more loving by not letting our pride rule our emotions.

Tip #41: Make him a Central Part of your Life

When you started dating, your life seems to revolve around him. You always think of him day and night. Your heart beats faster whenever you see him or talk to him. He seems to just complete your world and your happiness is to be with him!

This feeling shouldn't stop when you become a couple. But instead, it should become intense and grow much more!

Being your other half, you just have to make him the central part of your life. He deserves your attention more as you become a couple.

There are some couples who seem to lost the "feeling" when kids arrive or as the relationship grows older.

When the kids arrive, it is sometimes the tendency to prioritize the kids more than the husband. That is a big NO NO! The kids are there because of your Love for each other. DO NOT neglect your husband. He is still a priority. In fact, he must still be your No.1 priority.

As the relationship grows older, the more that your Love for each other must grow. You become a part of him and he becomes a part of you. You become one with him. So, in every decision that you make, always seek his opinions and make decisions as a couple.

Tip #42: Be Attentive to his Needs

As a wife, you have a role to fulfill to your husband. The need for sexual fulfilment is one of the important needs of a man.

One of the reasons why there is divorce, or separation is an unsatisfying sexual life together. (And as Grant discussed in Chapter 2... couples must have a sensual life together.)

Sex is one of man's basic needs. That's why couples decide to live together and become one.

Falling in Soul-Full Love Tips – Book 1

It is your duty as a wife to satisfy your husband sexually. Keep him at the comforts of your own home and that only you he will desire.

Do not give him the reason to look for other ways to satisfy his needs. Be always ready to give and to receive. It is with mutual understanding that you both satisfy your own needs.

Keep yourself clean just as you keep your home clean at all times.

Be always attractive to your husband.

He is the first and the last to see you every day, so always keep yourself beautiful for him.

It doesn't mean wearing makeup at all times, but a simple tidying up of oneself is all you need.

Sometimes when kids come, the wife tends to focus more on them and the needs of her husband become secondary.

Remember that your husband must still be your No.1 priority!

Show your love by simply keeping his things tidy and cooking his favorite meal.

By being attentive to his needs, you are making him Love you more every day.

Tip #43: Become his Best Friend and Lover

Be your husband's Best Friend. Keep each other's company at all times. Go wherever he goes. Go out and have fun together like friends would.

Be interested in his hobbies and share your hobbies with him.

Share and keep secrets with him.

Always be honest and trust him at all times. When in doubt, ask and confirm. Do not hold grudges.

Some couples start out as friends. As they get to know each other more, the relationship grows deeper. In such instances, do not break the bond of friendship. Because as friends, there are no pretentions and you are more open to one another.

A couple that started out as friends has usually a stronger bond than couples who started as lovers. Even so, attain to become your spouse's best friend.

Tip #44: Trust his Capability to Provide

The man's main role is to provide for the family. Trust him to do so.

If he cannot well provide for the family and you feel that he is struggling, learn to make ends meet.

Do not complain as it will just make things worse. Instead, thank him still for being able to provide.

Sometimes it takes just a little tightening of the budget.

When necessary, help him carry out his task. Give him a helping hand.

A good relationship is also a good partnership. Division of work and sharing of responsibilities are necessary.

I grew up in a family setting where the husband is the provider and the wife is the keeper of the house. But in these modern times, when the husband cannot provide well, the tendency is for the wife to also work and help with the finances.

When both parents work, the tendency is for the kids to be left in the care of the nannies or the grannies. However necessary, this is no longer the ideal typical family setting.

And the role of the husband is sometimes overruled. It may hurt his ego when the wife earns more. In such case, do not let pride sink in.

Be considerate of your husband's feelings.

Boost his ego by being grateful to him.

Always thank him for being able and trying to provide.

Make him feel that he is still the master of your heart and your home.

Tip #45: Be Loyal to him

Loyalty and Trust goes hand in hand and it keeps the relationship stronger.

To be able to be trusted, be a loyal partner.

Make him feel that he is the only man in your life, and really prove that he is.

There are times when the loyalty is challenged by circumstances. When financial difficulties arise, some women would work overseas to support the family.

Having gone far away from the husband, a long-distance relationship is hard to maintain.

Couples tend to break up due to this. Oftentimes, one or both parties become unfaithful to each other.

Falling in Soul-Full Love Tips – Book 1

I know a couple who have undergone really tough times together. It was their loyalty to each other that was challenged. It took a long time but the husband is always hopeful that someday his wife would come to her senses and return home.

And eventually, True Love finds its way home. Now they are back together and the family re-united.

Being a loyal partner is easy to do if you just keep your Love for him rule your heart and being considerate of his feelings.

Guard your heart from temptations.

Keep in mind that you have decided to Love him from the start.

Make that Love grow until the end of your Life together.

Falling in Soul-Full Love Tips – Book 1

"If you treat a man as he is,

He will stay as he is.

But if you treat him as if he were what he ought to be,

And could be,

He will become that bigger and better man."

-Goethe 1774

Chapter 7 – Putting It All Together

In this chapter, we work on putting all what we've learned in the previous chapters together and give you suggestions on how to turn these into new actions and then into new habits.

We've given you a lot of tips in this book. We don't expect you to try them all in a single day as that is not proper. Instead, try one or two a week. Do them multiple weeks and soon you will have a wonderful habit that you look forward to and then appreciate it when it arrives.

Soul-Full Love is a journey, a long, careful journey that leads to Forever. So, don't be in a haste. Slow and steady wins here. There are no fast lanes, no shortcuts. You can't

Falling in Soul-Full Love Tips – Book 1

trick or game Soul-Full Love. You have to let it proceed at its own measure pace, fast or slow as it will. And it's in that journey, free of schedules, deadlines, and Must-do's. Where you will find what you and your man are looking for.

Enjoy the journey!

   - Cary Grant Anderson and Christina Balingbing

And here are some final important Tips on the next few pages…

Falling in Soul-Full Love Tips – Book 1

Tip #46: Slow and Steady

We often seem to be in a hurry with Love. And lust. Often it is just the lust that drives us to hurry. Sometimes it's the hope that we've found The One. Fast can lead to a fast burn...And a fast burnout where each of you wonder what you are doing with the other now that the passion has burned down to ashes.

Well...That occasionally happens. Sometimes we are attracted to a person not because of the long-term potential but rather due to our need for something intangible that the other person has. The Passion brings you together, you energetically fulfill yourself and often each other, and...Then you're done. And, really, that is unfortunately that because now you've got what you needed on the inside from the other person, and vice versa, and you're going to need some time, some years, to really absorb and understand it. So Forever doesn't start right then unfortunately because you are not ready for it.

And you have to be Ready for Love, especially Soul-Full Love.

And sometimes you go too fast and...You crash. You went too fast and didn't make the curve and went careening off into the deep chasm...And so does the future of your Love in this instance.

So...Consider keeping it slow and steady. A measured pace. A walking pace. You want to make those curves in the road ahead. Slow down and don't let lust mess things up.

A technique that I've used that really helps reduce and tone down sexual excitement is very simple: Raise up the other person's left arm up over their head. Now press in gently but firmly just below the armpit and slightly to the rear. Hold it for about 30 – 60 seconds. And your other should calm right down. A bit gentler than a cold shower!

Remember...Slow and Steady.

Just walk hand in hand down a park or forest path...Talking. Slow and Steady.

Tip #47: Only One (or Two) Tips a Week!

In today's busy world we are now used to getting things IMMEDIATELY!

Well, Love doesn't just arrive when we order it from our cell phones like a delivery dinner.

And you can't develop skills and especially artful skills in just a day or two.

The Soul-Full Love Teachings of our School is really called the Soul-Full Love ARTS...Because it is an art form. And you are the Artist. And it will take some time to develop your skills and Soul-Full Love Arts forms.

So, try only one or two tips a week. Hopefully if you try two a week then those two will be similar or related so you can flow one into another.

Else...Just try one tip a week! There's 52 Tips here in this book so just do one each week.

Start at #1 and work your way through them all.

We also have a Soul-Full Love Tip of the Week email service on our website that you can sign up for. It will automatically send you a Soul-Full Love Tip to you via email once a week, so you can practice it that week.

Either way a Soul-Full Love Tip a week can be really, really fun!

Tip #48: Make Each Tip a Habit

It is said that when you practice something new for several weeks then it becomes a habit.

And we think that does work.

So, keep practicing the Tips that you have learned throughout the week.

You don't have to do all the Tips in a single week...Just mix them up a bit, randomly, so as to keep surprising your Love.

This lets you revisit previously learned tips and help make them a habit.

So, each week:

1. Learn and Practice a New Tip, and
2. Practice an Old Tip too!

And develop your own set of:

1. Everyday Tips
2. Some Time in the Week Tips
3. Randomly Applied to Keep Her/Him Guessing Tips.

It's a Challenge...And very Fun!

Tip #49: Restart Forgotten Tips Occasionally

While you practice a new Tip, each week don't forget the old Tips!

Think back over the previous Tips that you've learned and grab one and do it this week!

Remember to use temporarily forgotten Tips as Tips that you do randomly throughout the month, season, and year.

Keeping your Love guessing will keep the surprise and delight in your Soul-Full Loving.

Tip #50: Ride Through the Bumps in the Road

Life is always going to give us what I call "Bumps in the Road". These are things that we didn't expect or plan for. Most of the times we call them "problems". But sometimes, perhaps oftentimes, they are really Challenges. Challenges that we must meet as Heroes and Heroines to defeat and vanquish.

What would be Love, or Life, without an occasional Challenge or two?

So, get on your White Horse and ride through the Bumps in the Road.

And see if you can slide a Tip in there to surprise your Love too!

Tip #51: Forever is Long Time...There is No Hurry

When Forever is your goal...What is the rush?

Better to do it right, do it properly, and build something that lasts.

You Soul is going to survive the death of your body.

And your Love can too.

While we will write and teach more about this...

Look deep into your Love's eyes (eye gazing) and think about this topic...

And you'll Know that its true!

Your Soul-Full Love is an investment in yourself and another. It's an investment in Forever.

Forever is a long time...There is no hurry.

Tip #52: Enjoy the Journey!

Ok, it's time that I admit another one of my closely guarded secrets:

I love doing these Tips...
because...
they are so much Fun for me!

And I think that you will find them very fun too!

And remember this is the Soul-Full Love ARTS!

You're a Soul-Full Love Artist!

So, explore...Try variations...Each day is an opportunity for your Masterpiece...And each following is another chance to do even better!

Practice and hone your skills!

Take pride in your ability...But always try to improve a little better!

Get your Love into this fun game and see what he/she comes up with. Make it a game of Soul-Full Love Fun!

Enjoy the Journey!!!

- Cary Grant Anderson and Christina Balingbing

After Words

This book has been quite a journey for us. This book was Christina's idea and a very good idea it is indeed!

She has been very patient with me in getting me to complete the Chapters and Sections in this book as I get distracted a lot and also forget things far too often. She has kept me returning to complete this book especially when I forget about it.

I forget many, many things from time to time but I have never forgotten Christina for a single day. Though she lives on the other side of the planet from me as I write these words in 2016, she is always daily in my thoughts and in my mind. We are working towards being together each and every day and that will happen in the coming year (2017).

It has been a very long and difficult journey in life for both of us.

Life has probably been difficult for you as well. Just remember that Love, especially Soul-Full Love is always possible.

- Cary Grant Anderson

About the Soul-Full Love School™

The Soul-Full Love School™ was founded by Cary Grant Anderson and Christina Balingbing with a simple yet important mission – to teach the world how to Love... Soul-Fully.

The Soul-Full Love Arts are new ideas about Love and the Soul from a practical yet spiritual perspective. Love is something more than what many of us has been taught or have yet experienced. Learning the Arts and the Science of Soul-Full Love thru our website, our books and our courses. Love is what we all seek, and the Soul-Full Love Arts provides you data to learning and achieving the 3rd and highest level of Love – Soul-Full Love.

Join us at www.Soul-FullLove.School!

About the Triple Heart Logo

The triple hearts logo was created by Cary Grant Anderson to represent the Love between two people. Each person comes with heart, sometimes a little beaten or broken, and comes to Love to find Soul-Full fulfillment and completion. The Love that exists between two people forms a third heart – the Heart of Love. This Love is meant to warm our hearts and fill our Souls, so it can grow over the years into Forever Love.

Two Hearts...Into One!

The Soul-Full Love School™
www.Soul-FullLove.School

As the heart of Love grows, Souls touch and connect with the Other to become One Heart, One Love, One Soul... Forever.

About the Authors

Cary Grant Anderson is a brilliant Software Developer, Spiritual Theorist and a DaVinci Mind. He has a lot of books from light humor to deep spiritual theories that he is writing. He is the author and the brain behind Sentience.Life Concepts and Theory of which Soul-Full Love Theory is a major component.

The *Falling in Soul-Full Love Tips* book is a book series originating from Sentience.Life Concepts and Theory mixed with his personal experience and practices. He has been married several times and he's been a single father since 1994.

Grant, as he likes to be called, has a Bachelor's Degree in Economics, History, Computer Engineering, and Computer Science, and a Master's Degree in Transpersonal Psychology with specialization in Spiritual Psychology. He is currently pursuing a PhD in e Learning, as well as writing more books and developing courses in Soul-Full Love and Sentience.Life Theory.

Christina Balingbing is a native Bicolana from the southern Luzon province of the Philippines. This is her first Book co-authoring with the brilliant developer/author Cary Grant Anderson. Her ideas in this book are the result of the lessons learned from past relationships and her aspirations for an ideal Loving relationship.

Combined with Grant's beautiful notion of Love spelled with a capital "L", they have together written a book entitled *'Falling in Soul-Full Love Tips'*. This book was created to serve as a guide, a road map to a successful, healthier and more Loving relationships.

Ever since a child, she had always admired a complete happy family, where the couples Love each other very much. That was her dream to also have a complete happy family. She already had an idea on how it is going to be.

Meeting Grant made this dream realized. They both have similar experiences and values in life. Luckily also, they both have the same aspirations in life. To teach people how to Love and to share what they know.

Falling in Soul-Full Love Tips – Book 1

The Tips Book and Course Series

This is the beginning of the Tips book series.

There are 7 books and matching courses planned in the Soul-Full Love Tips series:

Book 1 – Beginnings

    Chapter 1 – Introduction
    Chapter 2 – Daily Love Duties
    Chapter 3 – Weekly Musts
    Chapter 4 – True Romance
    Chapter 5 – Honoring the Goddess (Woman)
    Chapter 6 – Honoring the Godden (Man)
    Chapter 7 – Putting It All Together

Book 2 – Knowing How to Love

    Chapter 1 – Introduction
    Chapter 2 – What Love is Not
    Chapter 3 – What Love Is
    Chapter 4 – What Loving Is
    Chapter 5 – The 3 Levels of Love
    Chapter 6 – Loving Soul-Fully
    Chapter 7 – Putting It All Together

Book 3 – Spirit-Full Sex

Chapter 1 – Introduction
Chapter 2 – Spirit-Full Defined
Chapter 3 – Spirit-Full Sex
Chapter 3 – Things to Avoid and Why
Chapter 5 – Honoring the Goddess (Woman) - Sexually
Chapter 6 – Honoring the Godden (Man) - Sexually
Chapter 7 – Putting It All Together

Book 4 – Having Fun Together!

Chapter 1 – Introduction
Chapter 2 – The Critical Importance of Having Fun!
Chapter 3 – Finding the Balance in Fun
Chapter 4 – Fun Things Together!
Chapter 5 – Fun Things for a Goddess Day!
Chapter 6 – Fun Things for a Godden Day!
Chapter 7 – Putting It All Together

Book 5 – Dealing with the Bumps in the Road

Chapter 1 – Introduction
Chapter 2 – Dealing with Bumps
Chapter 3 – Little Bumps
Chapter 4 – Big Bumps
Chapter 5 – Reconciling
Chapter 6 – When It's Time to Split
Chapter 7 – Putting It All Together

Book 6 – Going the Distance with Love

    Chapter 1 – Introduction
    Chapter 2 – Living Together Practically
    Chapter 3 – No Vices or Problems
    Chapter 4 – Living Together Sweetly
    Chapter 5 – Living Together Spirit-Fully
    Chapter 6 – Living Together Soul-Fully
    Chapter 7 – Putting It All Together

Book 7 – Forever Love (Sweet Music Together)

    Chapter 1 – Introduction
    Chapter 2 – Love…Forever
    Chapter 3 – Moving From Spirit-Full to Soul-Full
    Chapter 4 – Soul-Full Love
    Chapter 5 – Living Together Soul-Fully Together Forever
    Chapter 6 – Soul-Full Twynning
    Chapter 7 – Putting It All Together

Please visit our website at www.Soul-FullLove.School to learn more about them!

Made in the USA
Columbia, SC
08 January 2025